Jiu Jitsu Journal

DETAILS

NAME

ADDRESS

E-MAIL ADDRESS

WEBSITE

PHONE   **FAX**

EMERGENCY CONTACT PERSON

PHONE   **FAX**

Jiu Jitsu Journal

Date ....

WEEK

SESSION

INSTRUCTOR

WEIGHT

BELT RANK

☐ GI   ☐ NOGI   ☐ BOTH

TECHNIQUE #1

TECHNIQUE #2

TECHNIQUE #3

TRAINING PARTNERS

DRILLS

NOTES

TOTAL HOURS OF TRAINING

Jiu Jitsu Journal

Date ....

WEEK ....

SESSION ....

INSTRUCTOR ....

WEIGHT ....

BELT RANK ....

☐ GI   ☐ NOGI   ☐ BOTH

TECHNIQUE #1

TECHNIQUE #2

TECHNIQUE #3

TRAINING PARTNERS

DRILLS

NOTES

TOTAL HOURS OF TRAINING

Jiu Jitsu Journal

Date ....

WEEK _____   **SESSION** _____

INSTRUCTOR _____   **WEIGHT** _____

BELT RANK _____

☐ GI   ☐ NOGI   ☐ BOTH

TECHNIQUE #1

TECHNIQUE #2

TECHNIQUE #3

TRAINING PARTNERS

DRILLS

NOTES

TOTAL HOURS OF TRAINING _____

Jiu Jitsu Journal

Date ....

WEEK ████████████████ **SESSION** ████████████████

INSTRUCTOR ████████████ **WEIGHT** ████████████

BELT RANK ████████████ ☐ GI ☐ NOGI ☐ BOTH

TECHNIQUE #1

TECHNIQUE #2

TECHNIQUE #3

TRAINING PARTNERS

DRILLS

NOTES

TOTAL HOURS OF TRAINING

Jiu Jitsu Journal

Date ....

WEEK ▢▢▢▢▢▢▢▢▢▢   **SESSION** ▢▢▢▢▢▢▢▢

INSTRUCTOR ▢▢▢▢▢▢▢▢   **WEIGHT** ▢▢▢▢▢▢▢▢

BELT RANK ▢▢▢▢▢▢▢▢   ☐ **GI**   ☐ **NOGI**   ☐ **BOTH**

TECHNIQUE #1

TECHNIQUE #2

TECHNIQUE #3

TRAINING PARTNERS

DRILLS

NOTES

TOTAL HOURS OF TRAINING

Jiu Jitsu Journal

Date ....

WEEK _____   **SESSION** _____

INSTRUCTOR _____   **WEIGHT** _____

BELT RANK _____   ☐ GI   ☐ NOGI   ☐ BOTH

TECHNIQUE #1

TECHNIQUE #2

TECHNIQUE #3

TRAINING PARTNERS

DRILLS

NOTES

TOTAL HOURS OF TRAINING _____

Jiu Jitsu Journal

Date ....

WEEK _____ **SESSION** _____

INSTRUCTOR _____ **WEIGHT** _____

BELT RANK _____ ☐ GI ☐ NOGI ☐ BOTH

TECHNIQUE #1

TECHNIQUE #2

TECHNIQUE #3

TRAINING PARTNERS

DRILLS

NOTES

TOTAL HOURS OF TRAINING _____

Jiu Jitsu Journal

Date ....

WEEK .... SESSION ....

INSTRUCTOR .... WEIGHT ....

BELT RANK .... ☐ GI ☐ NOGI ☐ BOTH

TECHNIQUE #1

TECHNIQUE #2

TECHNIQUE #3

TRAINING PARTNERS

DRILLS

NOTES

TOTAL HOURS OF TRAINING ....

Jiu Jitsu Journal

Date ....

WEEK _____ **SESSION** _____

INSTRUCTOR _____ **WEIGHT** _____

BELT RANK _____ ☐ GI ☐ NOGI ☐ BOTH

TECHNIQUE #1

TECHNIQUE #2

TECHNIQUE #3

TRAINING PARTNERS

DRILLS

NOTES

TOTAL HOURS OF TRAINING _____

Jiu Jitsu Journal

Date ....

WEEK

SESSION

INSTRUCTOR

WEIGHT

BELT RANK

☐ GI   ☐ NOGI   ☐ BOTH

TECHNIQUE #1

TECHNIQUE #2

TECHNIQUE #3

TRAINING PARTNERS

DRILLS

NOTES

TOTAL HOURS OF TRAINING

Jiu Jitsu Journal

Date ....

WEEK _____ **SESSION** _____

INSTRUCTOR _____ **WEIGHT** _____

BELT RANK _____ ☐ GI ☐ NOGI ☐ BOTH

TECHNIQUE #1

TECHNIQUE #2

TECHNIQUE #3

TRAINING PARTNERS

DRILLS

NOTES

TOTAL HOURS OF TRAINING _____

Jiu Jitsu Journal

Date ....

WEEK .... SESSION ....

INSTRUCTOR .... WEIGHT ....

BELT RANK .... ☐ GI   ☐ NOGI   ☐ BOTH

TECHNIQUE #1

TECHNIQUE #2

TECHNIQUE #3

TRAINING PARTNERS

DRILLS

NOTES

TOTAL HOURS OF TRAINING

Jiu Jitsu Journal

Date ....

WEEK _____

SESSION _____

INSTRUCTOR _____

WEIGHT _____

BELT RANK _____

☐ GI ☐ NOGI ☐ BOTH

TECHNIQUE #1

TECHNIQUE #2

TECHNIQUE #3

TRAINING PARTNERS

DRILLS

NOTES

TOTAL HOURS OF TRAINING _____

Jiu Jitsu Journal

Date ....

WEEK ....

SESSION ....

INSTRUCTOR ....

WEIGHT ....

BELT RANK ....

☐ GI ☐ NOGI ☐ BOTH

TECHNIQUE #1

TECHNIQUE #2

TECHNIQUE #3

TRAINING PARTNERS

DRILLS

NOTES

TOTAL HOURS OF TRAINING

Jiu Jitsu Journal

Date ....

WEEK _____   **SESSION** _____

INSTRUCTOR _____   **WEIGHT** _____

BELT RANK _____   ☐ GI   ☐ NOGI   ☐ BOTH

TECHNIQUE #1

TECHNIQUE #2

TECHNIQUE #3

TRAINING PARTNERS

DRILLS

NOTES

TOTAL HOURS OF TRAINING _____

Jiu Jitsu Journal

Date ....

WEEK

INSTRUCTOR

BELT RANK

SESSION

WEIGHT

☐ GI   ☐ NOGI   ☐ BOTH

TECHNIQUE #1

TECHNIQUE #2

TECHNIQUE #3

TRAINING PARTNERS

DRILLS

NOTES

TOTAL HOURS OF TRAINING

Jiu Jitsu Journal

Date ....

WEEK _____ **SESSION** _____

INSTRUCTOR _____ **WEIGHT** _____

BELT RANK _____ ☐ GI ☐ NOGI ☐ BOTH

TECHNIQUE #1

TECHNIQUE #2

TECHNIQUE #3

TRAINING PARTNERS

DRILLS

NOTES

TOTAL HOURS OF TRAINING _____

Jiu Jitsu Journal

Date ....

WEEK

SESSION

INSTRUCTOR

WEIGHT

BELT RANK

☐ GI   ☐ NOGI   ☐ BOTH

TECHNIQUE #1

TECHNIQUE #2

TECHNIQUE #3

TRAINING PARTNERS

DRILLS

NOTES

TOTAL HOURS OF TRAINING

Jiu Jitsu Journal

Date ....

WEEK

INSTRUCTOR

BELT RANK

SESSION

WEIGHT

☐ GI ☐ NOGI ☐ BOTH

TECHNIQUE #1

TECHNIQUE #2

TECHNIQUE #3

TRAINING PARTNERS

DRILLS

NOTES

TOTAL HOURS OF TRAINING

Jiu Jitsu Journal

Date ....

WEEK

SESSION

INSTRUCTOR

WEIGHT

BELT RANK

☐ GI ☐ NOGI ☐ BOTH

TECHNIQUE #1

TECHNIQUE #2

TECHNIQUE #3

TRAINING PARTNERS

DRILLS

NOTES

TOTAL HOURS OF TRAINING

Jiu Jitsu Journal

Date ....

WEEK

SESSION

INSTRUCTOR

WEIGHT

BELT RANK

☐ GI   ☐ NOGI   ☐ BOTH

TECHNIQUE #1

TECHNIQUE #2

TECHNIQUE #3

TRAINING PARTNERS

DRILLS

NOTES

TOTAL HOURS OF TRAINING

Jiu Jitsu Journal

Date ....

WEEK _____   **SESSION** _____

INSTRUCTOR _____   **WEIGHT** _____

BELT RANK _____   ☐ GI   ☐ NOGI   ☐ BOTH

TECHNIQUE #1

TECHNIQUE #2

TECHNIQUE #3

TRAINING PARTNERS

DRILLS

NOTES

TOTAL HOURS OF TRAINING _____

Jiu Jitsu Journal

Date ....

WEEK _____   **SESSION** _____

INSTRUCTOR _____   **WEIGHT** _____

BELT RANK _____

☐ GI   ☐ NOGI   ☐ BOTH

TECHNIQUE #1

TECHNIQUE #2

TECHNIQUE #3

TRAINING PARTNERS

DRILLS

NOTES

TOTAL HOURS OF TRAINING _____

Jiu Jitsu Journal

Date ....

WEEK

SESSION

INSTRUCTOR

WEIGHT

BELT RANK

☐ GI   ☐ NOGI   ☐ BOTH

TECHNIQUE #1

TECHNIQUE #2

TECHNIQUE #3

TRAINING PARTNERS

DRILLS

NOTES

TOTAL HOURS OF TRAINING

Jiu Jitsu Journal

Date ....

WEEK _____   **SESSION** _____

INSTRUCTOR _____   **WEIGHT** _____

BELT RANK _____   ☐ GI   ☐ NOGI   ☐ BOTH

TECHNIQUE #1

TECHNIQUE #2

TECHNIQUE #3

TRAINING PARTNERS

DRILLS

NOTES

TOTAL HOURS OF TRAINING

Jiu Jitsu Journal

Date ....

WEEK

SESSION

INSTRUCTOR

WEIGHT

BELT RANK

☐ GI ☐ NOGI ☐ BOTH

TECHNIQUE #1

TECHNIQUE #2

TECHNIQUE #3

TRAINING PARTNERS

DRILLS

NOTES

TOTAL HOURS OF TRAINING

Jiu Jitsu Journal

Date ....

WEEK

SESSION

INSTRUCTOR

WEIGHT

BELT RANK

☐ GI   ☐ NOGI   ☐ BOTH

TECHNIQUE #1

TECHNIQUE #2

TECHNIQUE #3

TRAINING PARTNERS

DRILLS

NOTES

TOTAL HOURS OF TRAINING

Jiu Jitsu Journal

Date ....

WEEK

INSTRUCTOR

BELT RANK

SESSION

WEIGHT

☐ GI ☐ NOGI ☐ BOTH

TECHNIQUE #1

TECHNIQUE #2

TECHNIQUE #3

TRAINING PARTNERS

DRILLS

NOTES

TOTAL HOURS OF TRAINING

Jiu Jitsu Journal

Date ....

WEEK _____ **SESSION** _____

INSTRUCTOR _____ **WEIGHT** _____

BELT RANK _____ ☐ GI   ☐ NOGI   ☐ BOTH

TECHNIQUE #1

TECHNIQUE #2

TECHNIQUE #3

TRAINING PARTNERS

DRILLS

NOTES

TOTAL HOURS OF TRAINING

Jiu Jitsu Journal

Date ....

WEEK

SESSION

INSTRUCTOR

WEIGHT

BELT RANK

☐ GI   ☐ NOGI   ☐ BOTH

TECHNIQUE #1

TECHNIQUE #2

TECHNIQUE #3

TRAINING PARTNERS

DRILLS

NOTES

TOTAL HOURS OF TRAINING

Jiu Jitsu Journal

Date ....

WEEK

SESSION

INSTRUCTOR

WEIGHT

BELT RANK

☐ **GI**   ☐ **NOGI**   ☐ **BOTH**

TECHNIQUE #1

TECHNIQUE #2

TECHNIQUE #3

TRAINING PARTNERS

DRILLS

NOTES

TOTAL HOURS OF TRAINING

Jiu Jitsu Journal

Date ....

WEEK		**SESSION**	
INSTRUCTOR		**WEIGHT**	
BELT RANK		☐ GI ☐ NOGI ☐ BOTH	

TECHNIQUE #1

TECHNIQUE #2

TECHNIQUE #3

TRAINING PARTNERS

DRILLS

NOTES

TOTAL HOURS OF TRAINING

Jiu Jitsu Journal

Date ....

WEEK

SESSION

INSTRUCTOR

WEIGHT

BELT RANK

☐ GI ☐ NOGI ☐ BOTH

TECHNIQUE #1

TECHNIQUE #2

TECHNIQUE #3

TRAINING PARTNERS

DRILLS

NOTES

TOTAL HOURS OF TRAINING

Jiu Jitsu Journal

Date ....

WEEK ....   SESSION ....

INSTRUCTOR ....   WEIGHT ....

BELT RANK ....   ☐ GI   ☐ NOGI   ☐ BOTH

TECHNIQUE #1

TECHNIQUE #2

TECHNIQUE #3

TRAINING PARTNERS

DRILLS

NOTES

TOTAL HOURS OF TRAINING

Jiu Jitsu Journal

Date ....

WEEK

SESSION

INSTRUCTOR

WEIGHT

BELT RANK

☐ GI   ☐ NOGI   ☐ BOTH

TECHNIQUE #1

TECHNIQUE #2

TECHNIQUE #3

TRAINING PARTNERS

DRILLS

NOTES

TOTAL HOURS OF TRAINING

Jiu Jitsu Journal

Date ....

WEEK

SESSION

INSTRUCTOR

WEIGHT

BELT RANK

☐ GI ☐ NOGI ☐ BOTH

TECHNIQUE #1

TECHNIQUE #2

TECHNIQUE #3

TRAINING PARTNERS

DRILLS

NOTES

TOTAL HOURS OF TRAINING

Jiu Jitsu Journal

Date ....

WEEK _____   **SESSION** _____

INSTRUCTOR _____   **WEIGHT** _____

BELT RANK _____   ☐ GI   ☐ NOGI   ☐ BOTH

TECHNIQUE #1

TECHNIQUE #2

TECHNIQUE #3

TRAINING PARTNERS

DRILLS

NOTES

TOTAL HOURS OF TRAINING _____

Jiu Jitsu Journal

Date ....

WEEK _____   SESSION _____

INSTRUCTOR _____   WEIGHT _____

BELT RANK _____   ☐ GI   ☐ NOGI   ☐ BOTH

TECHNIQUE #1

TECHNIQUE #2

TECHNIQUE #3

TRAINING PARTNERS

DRILLS

NOTES

TOTAL HOURS OF TRAINING _____

Jiu Jitsu Journal

Date ....

WEEK _____   **SESSION** _____

INSTRUCTOR _____   **WEIGHT** _____

BELT RANK _____   ☐ GI   ☐ NOGI   ☐ BOTH

TECHNIQUE #1

TECHNIQUE #2

TECHNIQUE #3

TRAINING PARTNERS

DRILLS

NOTES

TOTAL HOURS OF TRAINING _____

Jiu Jitsu Journal

Date ....

WEEK .... SESSION ....

INSTRUCTOR .... WEIGHT ....

BELT RANK .... ☐ GI ☐ NOGI ☐ BOTH

TECHNIQUE #1

TECHNIQUE #2

TECHNIQUE #3

TRAINING PARTNERS

DRILLS

NOTES

TOTAL HOURS OF TRAINING ....

Jiu Jitsu Journal

Date ....

WEEK _____ **SESSION** _____

INSTRUCTOR _____ **WEIGHT** _____

BELT RANK _____ ☐ GI ☐ NOGI ☐ BOTH

TECHNIQUE #1

TECHNIQUE #2

TECHNIQUE #3

TRAINING PARTNERS

DRILLS

NOTES

TOTAL HOURS OF TRAINING _____

Jiu Jitsu Journal

Date ....

WEEK _____ **SESSION** _____

INSTRUCTOR _____ **WEIGHT** _____

BELT RANK _____ ☐ GI ☐ NOGI ☐ BOTH

TECHNIQUE #1

TECHNIQUE #2

TECHNIQUE #3

TRAINING PARTNERS

DRILLS

NOTES

TOTAL HOURS OF TRAINING _____

Jiu Jitsu Journal

Date ....

WEEK

SESSION

INSTRUCTOR

WEIGHT

BELT RANK

☐ GI ☐ NOGI ☐ BOTH

TECHNIQUE #1

TECHNIQUE #2

TECHNIQUE #3

TRAINING PARTNERS

DRILLS

NOTES

TOTAL HOURS OF TRAINING

Jiu Jitsu Journal

Date ....

WEEK .... SESSION ....

INSTRUCTOR .... WEIGHT ....

BELT RANK .... ☐ GI ☐ NOGI ☐ BOTH

TECHNIQUE #1

TECHNIQUE #2

TECHNIQUE #3

TRAINING PARTNERS

DRILLS

NOTES

TOTAL HOURS OF TRAINING

Jiu Jitsu Journal

Date ....

WEEK		SESSION	
INSTRUCTOR		**WEIGHT**	
BELT RANK			

☐ GI   ☐ NOGI   ☐ BOTH

TECHNIQUE #1

TECHNIQUE #2

TECHNIQUE #3

TRAINING PARTNERS

DRILLS

NOTES

TOTAL HOURS OF TRAINING

Jiu Jitsu Journal

Date ....

WEEK .... SESSION ....

INSTRUCTOR .... WEIGHT ....

BELT RANK .... ☐ GI ☐ NOGI ☐ BOTH

TECHNIQUE #1

TECHNIQUE #2

TECHNIQUE #3

TRAINING PARTNERS

DRILLS

NOTES

TOTAL HOURS OF TRAINING

Jiu Jitsu Journal

Date ....

WEEK

SESSION

INSTRUCTOR

WEIGHT

BELT RANK

☐ GI   ☐ NOGI   ☐ BOTH

TECHNIQUE #1

TECHNIQUE #2

TECHNIQUE #3

TRAINING PARTNERS

DRILLS

NOTES

TOTAL HOURS OF TRAINING

Jiu Jitsu Journal

Date ....

WEEK ....   SESSION ....

INSTRUCTOR ....   WEIGHT ....

BELT RANK ....   ☐ GI   ☐ NOGI   ☐ BOTH

TECHNIQUE #1

TECHNIQUE #2

TECHNIQUE #3

TRAINING PARTNERS

DRILLS

NOTES

TOTAL HOURS OF TRAINING

Jiu Jitsu Journal

Date ....

WEEK _____ **SESSION** _____

INSTRUCTOR _____ **WEIGHT** _____

BELT RANK _____ ☐ GI ☐ NOGI ☐ BOTH

TECHNIQUE #1

TECHNIQUE #2

TECHNIQUE #3

TRAINING PARTNERS

DRILLS

NOTES

TOTAL HOURS OF TRAINING _____

Jiu Jitsu Journal

Date ....

WEEK ....   SESSION ....

INSTRUCTOR ....   WEIGHT ....

BELT RANK ....   ☐ GI   ☐ NOGI   ☐ BOTH

TECHNIQUE #1

TECHNIQUE #2

TECHNIQUE #3

TRAINING PARTNERS

DRILLS

NOTES

TOTAL HOURS OF TRAINING

Jiu Jitsu Journal

Date ....

WEEK

INSTRUCTOR

BELT RANK

SESSION

WEIGHT

☐ GI   ☐ NOGI   ☐ BOTH

TECHNIQUE #1

TECHNIQUE #2

TECHNIQUE #3

TRAINING PARTNERS

DRILLS

NOTES

TOTAL HOURS OF TRAINING

Jiu Jitsu Journal

Date ....

WEEK

INSTRUCTOR

BELT RANK

SESSION

WEIGHT

☐ GI　　☐ NOGI　　☐ BOTH

TECHNIQUE #1

TECHNIQUE #2

TECHNIQUE #3

TRAINING PARTNERS

DRILLS

NOTES

TOTAL HOURS OF TRAINING

Jiu Jitsu Journal

Date ....

WEEK

SESSION

INSTRUCTOR

WEIGHT

BELT RANK

☐ GI ☐ NOGI ☐ BOTH

TECHNIQUE #1

TECHNIQUE #2

TECHNIQUE #3

TRAINING PARTNERS

DRILLS

NOTES

TOTAL HOURS OF TRAINING

Jiu Jitsu Journal

Date ....

WEEK

SESSION

INSTRUCTOR

WEIGHT

BELT RANK

☐ GI ☐ NOGI ☐ BOTH

TECHNIQUE #1

TECHNIQUE #2

TECHNIQUE #3

TRAINING PARTNERS

DRILLS

NOTES

TOTAL HOURS OF TRAINING

Jiu Jitsu Journal

Date ....

WEEK _____   **SESSION** _____

INSTRUCTOR _____   **WEIGHT** _____

BELT RANK _____   ☐ GI   ☐ NOGI   ☐ BOTH

TECHNIQUE #1

TECHNIQUE #2

TECHNIQUE #3

TRAINING PARTNERS

DRILLS

NOTES

TOTAL HOURS OF TRAINING _____

Jiu Jitsu Journal

Date ....

WEEK		**SESSION**	
INSTRUCTOR		**WEIGHT**	
BELT RANK			

☐ GI   ☐ NOGI   ☐ BOTH

TECHNIQUE #1

TECHNIQUE #2

TECHNIQUE #3

TRAINING PARTNERS

DRILLS

NOTES

TOTAL HOURS OF TRAINING

Jiu Jitsu Journal

Date ....

WEEK _____ **SESSION** _____

INSTRUCTOR _____ **WEIGHT** _____

BELT RANK _____ ☐ GI ☐ NOGI ☐ BOTH

TECHNIQUE #1

TECHNIQUE #2

TECHNIQUE #3

TRAINING PARTNERS

DRILLS

NOTES

TOTAL HOURS OF TRAINING _____

Jiu Jitsu Journal

Date ....

WEEK .... SESSION ....

INSTRUCTOR .... WEIGHT ....

BELT RANK .... ☐ GI ☐ NOGI ☐ BOTH

TECHNIQUE #1

TECHNIQUE #2

TECHNIQUE #3

TRAINING PARTNERS

DRILLS

NOTES

TOTAL HOURS OF TRAINING

Jiu Jitsu Journal

Date ....

WEEK

SESSION

INSTRUCTOR

WEIGHT

BELT RANK

☐ GI ☐ NOGI ☐ BOTH

TECHNIQUE #1

TECHNIQUE #2

TECHNIQUE #3

TRAINING PARTNERS

DRILLS

NOTES

TOTAL HOURS OF TRAINING

Jiu Jitsu Journal

Date ....

WEEK _____   **SESSION** _____

INSTRUCTOR _____   **WEIGHT** _____

BELT RANK _____   ☐ GI   ☐ NOGI   ☐ BOTH

TECHNIQUE #1

TECHNIQUE #2

TECHNIQUE #3

TRAINING PARTNERS

DRILLS

NOTES

TOTAL HOURS OF TRAINING _____

Jiu Jitsu Journal

Date ....

WEEK _____   **SESSION** _____

INSTRUCTOR _____   **WEIGHT** _____

BELT RANK _____   ☐ GI   ☐ NOGI   ☐ BOTH

TECHNIQUE #1

TECHNIQUE #2

TECHNIQUE #3

TRAINING PARTNERS

DRILLS

NOTES

TOTAL HOURS OF TRAINING _____

Jiu Jitsu Journal

Date ....

WEEK

SESSION

INSTRUCTOR

WEIGHT

BELT RANK

☐ GI   ☐ NOGI   ☐ BOTH

TECHNIQUE #1

TECHNIQUE #2

TECHNIQUE #3

TRAINING PARTNERS

DRILLS

NOTES

TOTAL HOURS OF TRAINING

Jiu Jitsu Journal

Date ....

WEEK ⬚⬚⬚⬚⬚⬚⬚⬚ **SESSION** ⬚⬚⬚⬚⬚⬚⬚

INSTRUCTOR ⬚⬚⬚⬚⬚⬚ **WEIGHT** ⬚⬚⬚⬚⬚⬚

BELT RANK ⬚⬚⬚⬚⬚⬚ ☐ GI ☐ NOGI ☐ BOTH

TECHNIQUE #1

TECHNIQUE #2

TECHNIQUE #3

TRAINING PARTNERS

DRILLS

NOTES

TOTAL HOURS OF TRAINING

Jiu Jitsu Journal

Date ....

WEEK		**SESSION**	
INSTRUCTOR		**WEIGHT**	
BELT RANK		☐ GI ☐ NOGI ☐ BOTH	

TECHNIQUE #1

TECHNIQUE #2

TECHNIQUE #3

TRAINING PARTNERS

DRILLS

NOTES

TOTAL HOURS OF TRAINING

Jiu Jitsu Journal

Date ....

WEEK

INSTRUCTOR

BELT RANK

SESSION

WEIGHT

☐ GI   ☐ NOGI   ☐ BOTH

TECHNIQUE #1

TECHNIQUE #2

TECHNIQUE #3

TRAINING PARTNERS

DRILLS

NOTES

TOTAL HOURS OF TRAINING

Jiu Jitsu Journal

Date ....

WEEK		**SESSION**	
INSTRUCTOR		**WEIGHT**	
BELT RANK		☐ GI ☐ NOGI ☐ BOTH	

TECHNIQUE #1

TECHNIQUE #2

TECHNIQUE #3

TRAINING PARTNERS

DRILLS

NOTES

TOTAL HOURS OF TRAINING

Jiu Jitsu Journal

Date ....

WEEK ▢▢▢   **SESSION** ▢▢▢

INSTRUCTOR ▢▢▢   **WEIGHT** ▢▢▢

BELT RANK ▢▢▢   ☐ GI   ☐ NOGI   ☐ BOTH

TECHNIQUE #1

TECHNIQUE #2

TECHNIQUE #3

TRAINING PARTNERS

DRILLS

NOTES

TOTAL HOURS OF TRAINING

Jiu Jitsu Journal

Date ....

WEEK

SESSION

INSTRUCTOR

WEIGHT

BELT RANK

☐ GI   ☐ NOGI   ☐ BOTH

TECHNIQUE #1

TECHNIQUE #2

TECHNIQUE #3

TRAINING PARTNERS

DRILLS

NOTES

TOTAL HOURS OF TRAINING

Jiu Jitsu Journal

Date ....

WEEK

SESSION

INSTRUCTOR

WEIGHT

BELT RANK

☐ GI   ☐ NOGI   ☐ BOTH

TECHNIQUE #1

TECHNIQUE #2

TECHNIQUE #3

TRAINING PARTNERS

DRILLS

NOTES

TOTAL HOURS OF TRAINING

Jiu Jitsu Journal

Date ....

WEEK _____ **SESSION** _____

INSTRUCTOR _____ **WEIGHT** _____

BELT RANK _____ ☐ GI ☐ NOGI ☐ BOTH

TECHNIQUE #1

TECHNIQUE #2

TECHNIQUE #3

TRAINING PARTNERS

DRILLS

NOTES

TOTAL HOURS OF TRAINING

Jiu Jitsu Journal

Date ....

WEEK _____

SESSION _____

INSTRUCTOR _____

WEIGHT _____

BELT RANK _____

☐ GI   ☐ NOGI   ☐ BOTH

TECHNIQUE #1

TECHNIQUE #2

TECHNIQUE #3

TRAINING PARTNERS

DRILLS

NOTES

TOTAL HOURS OF TRAINING _____

Jiu Jitsu Journal

Date ....

WEEK .... SESSION ....

INSTRUCTOR .... WEIGHT ....

BELT RANK .... ☐ GI ☐ NOGI ☐ BOTH

TECHNIQUE #1

TECHNIQUE #2

TECHNIQUE #3

TRAINING PARTNERS

DRILLS

NOTES

TOTAL HOURS OF TRAINING

Jiu Jitsu Journal

Date ....

WEEK _____ **SESSION** _____

INSTRUCTOR _____ **WEIGHT** _____

BELT RANK _____ ☐ GI ☐ NOGI ☐ BOTH

TECHNIQUE #1

TECHNIQUE #2

TECHNIQUE #3

TRAINING PARTNERS

DRILLS

NOTES

TOTAL HOURS OF TRAINING _____

Jiu Jitsu Journal

Date ....

WEEK _____   **SESSION** _____

INSTRUCTOR _____   **WEIGHT** _____

BELT RANK _____   ☐ GI   ☐ NOGI   ☐ BOTH

TECHNIQUE #1

TECHNIQUE #2

TECHNIQUE #3

TRAINING PARTNERS

DRILLS

NOTES

TOTAL HOURS OF TRAINING _____

Jiu Jitsu Journal

Date ....

WEEK _____ **SESSION** _____

INSTRUCTOR _____ **WEIGHT** _____

BELT RANK _____ ☐ GI ☐ NOGI ☐ BOTH

TECHNIQUE #1

TECHNIQUE #2

TECHNIQUE #3

TRAINING PARTNERS

DRILLS

NOTES

TOTAL HOURS OF TRAINING _____

Jiu Jitsu Journal

Date ....

WEEK

INSTRUCTOR

BELT RANK

SESSION

WEIGHT

☐ GI   ☐ NOGI   ☐ BOTH

TECHNIQUE #1

TECHNIQUE #2

TECHNIQUE #3

TRAINING PARTNERS

DRILLS

NOTES

TOTAL HOURS OF TRAINING

Jiu Jitsu Journal

Date ....

WEEK

SESSION

INSTRUCTOR

WEIGHT

BELT RANK

☐ GI   ☐ NOGI   ☐ BOTH

TECHNIQUE #1

TECHNIQUE #2

TECHNIQUE #3

TRAINING PARTNERS

DRILLS

NOTES

TOTAL HOURS OF TRAINING

Jiu Jitsu Journal

Date ....

WEEK _____   **SESSION** _____

INSTRUCTOR _____   **WEIGHT** _____

BELT RANK _____   ☐ GI   ☐ NOGI   ☐ BOTH

TECHNIQUE #1

TECHNIQUE #2

TECHNIQUE #3

TRAINING PARTNERS

DRILLS

NOTES

TOTAL HOURS OF TRAINING _____

Jiu Jitsu Journal

Date ....

WEEK _____ **SESSION** _____

INSTRUCTOR _____ **WEIGHT** _____

BELT RANK _____ ☐ GI ☐ NOGI ☐ BOTH

TECHNIQUE #1

TECHNIQUE #2

TECHNIQUE #3

TRAINING PARTNERS

DRILLS

NOTES

TOTAL HOURS OF TRAINING _____

Jiu Jitsu Journal

Date ....

WEEK _____ **SESSION** _____

INSTRUCTOR _____ **WEIGHT** _____

BELT RANK _____ ☐ GI ☐ NOGI ☐ BOTH

TECHNIQUE #1

TECHNIQUE #2

TECHNIQUE #3

TRAINING PARTNERS

DRILLS

NOTES

TOTAL HOURS OF TRAINING

Jiu Jitsu Journal

Date ....

WEEK _____   **SESSION** _____

INSTRUCTOR _____   **WEIGHT** _____

BELT RANK _____   ☐ GI   ☐ NOGI   ☐ BOTH

TECHNIQUE #1

TECHNIQUE #2

TECHNIQUE #3

TRAINING PARTNERS

DRILLS

NOTES

TOTAL HOURS OF TRAINING _____

Jiu Jitsu Journal

Date ....

WEEK

INSTRUCTOR

BELT RANK

SESSION

WEIGHT

☐ GI ☐ NOGI ☐ BOTH

TECHNIQUE #1

TECHNIQUE #2

TECHNIQUE #3

TRAINING PARTNERS

DRILLS

NOTES

TOTAL HOURS OF TRAINING

Jiu Jitsu Journal

Date ....

WEEK _____   **SESSION** _____

INSTRUCTOR _____   **WEIGHT** _____

BELT RANK _____   ☐ GI   ☐ NOGI   ☐ BOTH

TECHNIQUE #1

TECHNIQUE #2

TECHNIQUE #3

TRAINING PARTNERS

DRILLS

NOTES

TOTAL HOURS OF TRAINING _____

Jiu Jitsu Journal

Date ....

WEEK _____   **SESSION** _____

INSTRUCTOR _____   **WEIGHT** _____

BELT RANK _____   ☐ GI   ☐ NOGI   ☐ BOTH

TECHNIQUE #1

TECHNIQUE #2

TECHNIQUE #3

TRAINING PARTNERS

DRILLS

NOTES

TOTAL HOURS OF TRAINING _____

Jiu Jitsu Journal

Date ....

WEEK _____ **SESSION** _____

INSTRUCTOR _____ **WEIGHT** _____

BELT RANK _____ ☐ GI ☐ NOGI ☐ BOTH

TECHNIQUE #1

TECHNIQUE #2

TECHNIQUE #3

TRAINING PARTNERS

DRILLS

NOTES

TOTAL HOURS OF TRAINING _____

Jiu Jitsu Journal

Date ....

WEEK _____   **SESSION** _____

INSTRUCTOR _____   **WEIGHT** _____

BELT RANK _____   ☐ GI   ☐ NOGI   ☐ BOTH

TECHNIQUE #1

TECHNIQUE #2

TECHNIQUE #3

TRAINING PARTNERS

DRILLS

NOTES

TOTAL HOURS OF TRAINING

Jiu Jitsu Journal

Date ....

WEEK _____   **SESSION** _____

INSTRUCTOR _____   **WEIGHT** _____

BELT RANK _____   ☐ GI ☐ NOGI ☐ BOTH

TECHNIQUE #1

TECHNIQUE #2

TECHNIQUE #3

TRAINING PARTNERS

DRILLS

NOTES

TOTAL HOURS OF TRAINING _____

Jiu Jitsu Journal

Date ....

WEEK

SESSION

INSTRUCTOR

WEIGHT

BELT RANK

☐ GI ☐ NOGI ☐ BOTH

TECHNIQUE #1

TECHNIQUE #2

TECHNIQUE #3

TRAINING PARTNERS

DRILLS

NOTES

TOTAL HOURS OF TRAINING

Jiu Jitsu Journal

Date ....

WEEK

SESSION

INSTRUCTOR

WEIGHT

BELT RANK

☐ GI ☐ NOGI ☐ BOTH

TECHNIQUE #1

TECHNIQUE #2

TECHNIQUE #3

TRAINING PARTNERS

DRILLS

NOTES

TOTAL HOURS OF TRAINING

Jiu Jitsu Journal

Date ....

WEEK _____   **SESSION** _____

INSTRUCTOR _____   **WEIGHT** _____

BELT RANK _____   ☐ GI   ☐ NOGI   ☐ BOTH

TECHNIQUE #1

TECHNIQUE #2

TECHNIQUE #3

TRAINING PARTNERS

DRILLS

NOTES

TOTAL HOURS OF TRAINING _____

Jiu Jitsu Journal

Date ....

WEEK _____ **SESSION** _____

INSTRUCTOR _____ **WEIGHT** _____

BELT RANK _____ ☐ GI   ☐ NOGI   ☐ BOTH

TECHNIQUE #1

TECHNIQUE #2

TECHNIQUE #3

TRAINING PARTNERS

DRILLS

NOTES

TOTAL HOURS OF TRAINING _____

Jiu Jitsu Journal

Date ....

WEEK .... SESSION ....

INSTRUCTOR .... WEIGHT ....

BELT RANK .... ☐ GI ☐ NOGI ☐ BOTH

TECHNIQUE #1

TECHNIQUE #2

TECHNIQUE #3

TRAINING PARTNERS

DRILLS

NOTES

TOTAL HOURS OF TRAINING

Jiu Jitsu Journal

Date ....

WEEK

SESSION

INSTRUCTOR

WEIGHT

BELT RANK

☐ GI   ☐ NOGI   ☐ BOTH

TECHNIQUE #1

TECHNIQUE #2

TECHNIQUE #3

TRAINING PARTNERS

DRILLS

NOTES

TOTAL HOURS OF TRAINING

Jiu Jitsu Journal

Date ....

WEEK

SESSION

INSTRUCTOR

WEIGHT

BELT RANK

☐ GI   ☐ NOGI   ☐ BOTH

TECHNIQUE #1

TECHNIQUE #2

TECHNIQUE #3

TRAINING PARTNERS

DRILLS

NOTES

TOTAL HOURS OF TRAINING

Jiu Jitsu Journal

Date ....

WEEK

SESSION

INSTRUCTOR

WEIGHT

BELT RANK

☐ GI   ☐ NOGI   ☐ BOTH

TECHNIQUE #1

TECHNIQUE #2

TECHNIQUE #3

TRAINING PARTNERS

DRILLS

NOTES

TOTAL HOURS OF TRAINING

Jiu Jitsu Journal

Date ....

WEEK

INSTRUCTOR

BELT RANK

SESSION

WEIGHT

☐ GI   ☐ NOGI   ☐ BOTH

TECHNIQUE #1

TECHNIQUE #2

TECHNIQUE #3

TRAINING PARTNERS

DRILLS

NOTES

TOTAL HOURS OF TRAINING

Jiu Jitsu Journal

Date ....

WEEK _____   **SESSION** _____

INSTRUCTOR _____   **WEIGHT** _____

BELT RANK _____   ☐ GI   ☐ NOGI   ☐ BOTH

TECHNIQUE #1

TECHNIQUE #2

TECHNIQUE #3

TRAINING PARTNERS

DRILLS

NOTES

TOTAL HOURS OF TRAINING _____

Jiu Jitsu Journal

Date ....

WEEK _____ **SESSION** _____

INSTRUCTOR _____ **WEIGHT** _____

BELT RANK _____ ☐ GI ☐ NOGI ☐ BOTH

TECHNIQUE #1

TECHNIQUE #2

TECHNIQUE #3

TRAINING PARTNERS

DRILLS

NOTES

TOTAL HOURS OF TRAINING _____

Jiu Jitsu Journal

Date ....

WEEK _____   **SESSION** _____

INSTRUCTOR _____   **WEIGHT** _____

BELT RANK _____   ☐ GI   ☐ NOGI   ☐ BOTH

TECHNIQUE #1

TECHNIQUE #2

TECHNIQUE #3

TRAINING PARTNERS

DRILLS

NOTES

TOTAL HOURS OF TRAINING _____

Jiu Jitsu Journal

Date ....

WEEK

SESSION

INSTRUCTOR

WEIGHT

BELT RANK

☐ GI   ☐ NOGI   ☐ BOTH

TECHNIQUE #1

TECHNIQUE #2

TECHNIQUE #3

TRAINING PARTNERS

DRILLS

NOTES

TOTAL HOURS OF TRAINING

Jiu Jitsu Journal

Date ....

WEEK

SESSION

INSTRUCTOR

WEIGHT

BELT RANK

☐ GI ☐ NOGI ☐ BOTH

TECHNIQUE #1

TECHNIQUE #2

TECHNIQUE #3

TRAINING PARTNERS

DRILLS

NOTES

TOTAL HOURS OF TRAINING

Jiu Jitsu Journal

Date ....

WEEK _____   **SESSION** _____

INSTRUCTOR _____   **WEIGHT** _____

BELT RANK _____   ☐ GI ☐ NOGI ☐ BOTH

TECHNIQUE #1

TECHNIQUE #2

TECHNIQUE #3

TRAINING PARTNERS

DRILLS

NOTES

TOTAL HOURS OF TRAINING _____

Jiu Jitsu Journal

Date ....

WEEK _____

SESSION _____

INSTRUCTOR _____

WEIGHT _____

BELT RANK _____

☐ GI ☐ NOGI ☐ BOTH

TECHNIQUE #1

TECHNIQUE #2

TECHNIQUE #3

TRAINING PARTNERS

DRILLS

NOTES

TOTAL HOURS OF TRAINING _____

Jiu Jitsu Journal

Date ....

WEEK

SESSION

INSTRUCTOR

WEIGHT

BELT RANK

☐ GI ☐ NOGI ☐ BOTH

TECHNIQUE #1

TECHNIQUE #2

TECHNIQUE #3

TRAINING PARTNERS

DRILLS

NOTES

TOTAL HOURS OF TRAINING

Jiu Jitsu Journal

Date ....

WEEK

SESSION

INSTRUCTOR

WEIGHT

BELT RANK

☐ GI   ☐ NOGI   ☐ BOTH

TECHNIQUE #1

TECHNIQUE #2

TECHNIQUE #3

TRAINING PARTNERS

DRILLS

NOTES

TOTAL HOURS OF TRAINING

Jiu Jitsu Journal

Date ....

WEEK

SESSION

INSTRUCTOR

WEIGHT

BELT RANK

☐ GI ☐ NOGI ☐ BOTH

TECHNIQUE #1

TECHNIQUE #2

TECHNIQUE #3

TRAINING PARTNERS

DRILLS

NOTES

TOTAL HOURS OF TRAINING

Jiu Jitsu Journal

Date ....

WEEK

SESSION

INSTRUCTOR

WEIGHT

BELT RANK

☐ GI   ☐ NOGI   ☐ BOTH

TECHNIQUE #1

TECHNIQUE #2

TECHNIQUE #3

TRAINING PARTNERS

DRILLS

NOTES

TOTAL HOURS OF TRAINING

Jiu Jitsu Journal

Date ....

WEEK

INSTRUCTOR

BELT RANK

SESSION

WEIGHT

☐ GI ☐ NOGI ☐ BOTH

TECHNIQUE #1

TECHNIQUE #2

TECHNIQUE #3

TRAINING PARTNERS

DRILLS

NOTES

TOTAL HOURS OF TRAINING

Jiu Jitsu Journal

Date ....

WEEK   **SESSION**

INSTRUCTOR   **WEIGHT**

BELT RANK   ☐ **GI**   ☐ **NOGI**   ☐ **BOTH**

TECHNIQUE #1

TECHNIQUE #2

TECHNIQUE #3

TRAINING PARTNERS

DRILLS

NOTES

TOTAL HOURS OF TRAINING

Jiu Jitsu Journal

Date ....

WEEK _____   **SESSION** _____

INSTRUCTOR _____   **WEIGHT** _____

BELT RANK _____   ☐ GI   ☐ NOGI   ☐ BOTH

TECHNIQUE #1

TECHNIQUE #2

TECHNIQUE #3

TRAINING PARTNERS

DRILLS

NOTES

TOTAL HOURS OF TRAINING _____

Jiu Jitsu Journal

Date ....

WEEK

SESSION

INSTRUCTOR

WEIGHT

BELT RANK

☐ GI ☐ NOGI ☐ BOTH

TECHNIQUE #1

TECHNIQUE #2

TECHNIQUE #3

TRAINING PARTNERS

DRILLS

NOTES

TOTAL HOURS OF TRAINING

Jiu Jitsu Journal

Date ....

WEEK _____ **SESSION** _____

INSTRUCTOR _____ **WEIGHT** _____

BELT RANK _____ ☐ GI ☐ NOGI ☐ BOTH

TECHNIQUE #1

TECHNIQUE #2

TECHNIQUE #3

TRAINING PARTNERS

DRILLS

NOTES

TOTAL HOURS OF TRAINING _____

Jiu Jitsu Journal

Date ....

WEEK

SESSION

INSTRUCTOR

WEIGHT

BELT RANK

☐ GI   ☐ NOGI   ☐ BOTH

TECHNIQUE #1

TECHNIQUE #2

TECHNIQUE #3

TRAINING PARTNERS

DRILLS

NOTES

TOTAL HOURS OF TRAINING

Jiu Jitsu Journal

Date ....

WEEK

INSTRUCTOR

BELT RANK

SESSION

WEIGHT

☐ GI   ☐ NOGI   ☐ BOTH

TECHNIQUE #1

TECHNIQUE #2

TECHNIQUE #3

TRAINING PARTNERS

DRILLS

NOTES

TOTAL HOURS OF TRAINING

Jiu Jitsu Journal

Date ....

WEEK _____   SESSION _____

INSTRUCTOR _____   WEIGHT _____

BELT RANK _____   ☐ GI ☐ NOGI ☐ BOTH

TECHNIQUE #1

TECHNIQUE #2

TECHNIQUE #3

TRAINING PARTNERS

DRILLS

NOTES

TOTAL HOURS OF TRAINING _____

Jiu Jitsu Journal

Date ....

WEEK

SESSION

INSTRUCTOR

WEIGHT

BELT RANK

☐ GI   ☐ NOGI   ☐ BOTH

TECHNIQUE #1

TECHNIQUE #2

TECHNIQUE #3

TRAINING PARTNERS

DRILLS

NOTES

TOTAL HOURS OF TRAINING

Jiu Jitsu Journal

Date ....

WEEK _____ **SESSION** _____

INSTRUCTOR _____ **WEIGHT** _____

BELT RANK _____ ☐ GI ☐ NOGI ☐ BOTH

TECHNIQUE #1

TECHNIQUE #2

TECHNIQUE #3

TRAINING PARTNERS

DRILLS

NOTES

TOTAL HOURS OF TRAINING _____

Jiu Jitsu Journal

Date ....

WEEK ▢▢▢▢▢▢▢▢▢▢▢
SESSION ▢▢▢▢▢▢▢▢▢▢▢

INSTRUCTOR ▢▢▢▢▢▢▢▢▢▢▢
WEIGHT ▢▢▢▢▢▢▢▢▢▢▢

BELT RANK ▢▢▢▢▢▢▢▢▢▢▢

☐ GI   ☐ NOGI   ☐ BOTH

TECHNIQUE #1

TECHNIQUE #2

TECHNIQUE #3

TRAINING PARTNERS

DRILLS

NOTES

TOTAL HOURS OF TRAINING

Jiu Jitsu Journal

Date ....

WEEK _____   **SESSION** _____

INSTRUCTOR _____   **WEIGHT** _____

BELT RANK _____   ☐ GI   ☐ NOGI   ☐ BOTH

TECHNIQUE #1

TECHNIQUE #2

TECHNIQUE #3

TRAINING PARTNERS

DRILLS

NOTES

TOTAL HOURS OF TRAINING _____

Made in the USA
Las Vegas, NV
03 February 2024

85242073R00068